Going for the
Gold

Going for the Gold

Gold

Winning the Gold Medal
for Financial Independence

Lesley D. Bissett, CFP

OUACHITA TECHNICAL COLLEGE

SkillPath Publications
Mission, Kansas

Project Editor: Kelly Scanlon

Editor: Jane Doyle Guthrie

Cover and Book Design: Rod Hankins

ISBN: 1-57294-001-8

Library of Congress Catalog Card Number: 95-72994

10   9   8   7   6   00

Printed in the United States of America

To the three young men who have made me the
most fortunate person in the world—my sons John,
Richard, and Tom. How did I get so lucky.

Contents

Someday You'll Be Able to Look Back...

You're looking at a former Sleeping Beauty. For 16 years, I was a competitive and professional figure skater. I skated in competitions throughout Canada (including the Canadian Championships) for eight years, turned professional, and was a professional figure skater for eight years. For the last five years of my professional skating career, I was a featured performer with Shipstads and Johnson's Ice Follies, touring 48 weeks of the year to 22 cities in Canada and the United States. One of the reasons I took up figure skating as a young girl was because I wanted to wear pretty costumes. I lived that dream each year that I skated—the costumes in the Ice Follies were valued at several million dollars.

The fairy tale continued when I left Ice Follies in 1961 to marry a handsome television newscaster. Our engagement, our wedding, and the births of our three sons were all television events.

Only one day ten years later in 1972, Sleeping Beauty woke up and Prince Charming wasn't there. I was left with three children and very little money coming in. Agonizing over my near-poverty situation with the minister of my church I asked, "How am I going to support these children? Why has this happened to me?"

The minister replied, "I don't know. But someday you will be able to look back and understand the reason."

And he was right! By luck I got a job in the financial services world, and it was there I learned about this important topic called "financial planning." Less than a year later I told one of the financial advisors that I felt I had a message to deliver—and the message is this: "Don't be a Sleeping Beauty like me. Take an active interest in the family's finances so that if you lose a spouse through death or divorce, you won't have a financial trauma on top of an emotional one."

Since 1973 I have been delivering this message as one who woke up and survived. By reading this book, you're taking the first steps to setting yourself up to be healthy—financially, emotionally, and physically.

one

The Past: Are You Skating on Thin Ice?

Athletes like to view the videos of their past performances to see how they can correct, plan, and improve their future performances. So consider yourself a financial athlete who's going to begin training for the financial Olympic performance of your life. You're going to set the wheels in motion and plan for that glorious moment when you receive the gold medal for planning, technical merit, and performance of financial well-being. Your coach knows you can do it! Be prepared to fall occasionally—you've slipped or stumbled a few times already, right? That's okay.

Just think of how many bruised knees, chipped elbows, falls, stumbles, and missed take-offs skaters must have experienced before successfully landing their first multirevolution jump. A coach's favorite expressions are:

"Get up and try it again!"

"You're getting closer!"

"I know you can do it!"

Those who are successful financially *do* say these phrases to themselves. Knowing that *negative thoughts attract negative results*, these people become experts at positive self-talk to ensure positive results. In order to be successful in the future, you must look at your past mistakes and *learn* from them. In her tape *Success Through Self Confidence*, Beverly Nadler says, "There are no failures—only lessons." Successful people understand that to achieve success, they must let their past mistakes show them where *not* to go as well as identify the right course of action to reach their goals. It's always amazing to see the thousands of people who never learn from the past. You can assess your current and past financial habits by completing the quiz on the next page.

Quiz

Looking at Your Financial Habits

Build a picture of your past as a strategy for planning your future.

	Yes	No
1. Do you spend money to feel better?	____	____
2. Would you buy a suit that was a size too small because "it was a really good buy (on sale)" and it would motivate you to lose the ten pounds you've been wanting to lose?	____	____
3. Do you often add items to your grocery cart from the nearby racks as you're standing in line to check out?	____	____
4. Have you ever declared or thought of declaring bankruptcy?	____	____
5. When buying a car or other large item, have you ever allowed the salesperson to talk you into buying additional items (gold trim package, ice maker, etc.) that you really didn't want?	____	____
6. Do you go grocery shopping without a list?	____	____
7. If you do have a list, do you stray from it?	____	____
8. Would you buy eighty pounds of dog food for your pet Chihuahua because you got a really good deal at a discount store?	____	____

	Yes	No

9. When someone tries to sell you something on the phone, do you listen to the entire sales pitch rather than politely cutting off the conversation? _____ _____

10. Do you pay for something you really shouldn't buy by putting it on your credit card and then justify the purchase by saying, "It's only $200 for the next twenty-four months"? _____ _____

11. Have you ever maxed out your credit card(s) to make a down payment on an item? _____ _____

12. Except for home and auto, would you like to have all your bills paid off by the end of this year? _____ _____

13. Are you securing information about a bill consolidation loan? _____ _____

14. Have you ever used one credit card to pay off another? _____ _____

15. Do you consistently pay the minimum due on each of your credit cards? _____ _____

16. Do you have more than three credit cards? _____ _____

17. When purchasing gifts for special occasions, do you do so without establishing a limit for each gift that you buy? _____ _____

18. Do you find yourself saying, "Oh well! It's only money!" _____ _____

	Yes	No
19. Do you plan for Social Security payments to provide a substantial portion of your retirement income?	____	____
20. Do you find yourself constantly using the phrases, "When my ship comes in…" or "When I win the lottery…"?	____	____

Now, tally up the number of times you answered "yes" and see the message within your total:

1-2 **Put on a lifejacket—you're on thin ice!**

3-5 **Quick! Turn around—you're headed for disaster!**

5 or more **Call 911! You've fallen through and you're in trouble!**

Going for the gold is like driving down a highway. If you discover you're on the wrong highway, what do you do? Hopefully, you'll take the next exit and look at a map or ask for directions. You may have to detour and backtrack, but eventually you'll find the right road. Too many people for some reason *continue to stay on the wrong road!* They realize it, they say, "Gee! I guess I'm on the wrong road," and then simply keep going!

To achieve financial success (or any kind of success), you must accept that the road will not always be easy to follow. There will be twists, turns, potholes, detours, areas "under construction," bumps, hills, valleys, steep inclines, and sometimes four-lane freeways with a commuter lane. Good financial athletes aren't surprised by detours, bumps, inclines, and rough patches; they *expect* them and can deal with them if they appear. If the road is clear, so much the better. People get into financial trouble because they expect a divided four-lane freeway all the way. Life (and money) isn't like that.

two

The Present: What Shape Are You in Now?

W hat is your present financial condition? You can find out fairly easily by doing some "warm-up" exercises. Before you begin, remember one thing—be positive! As you complete these exercises, don't think: "Oh, good grief! I'm in terrible shape!" Instead, say to yourself: "This is the beginning of something wonderful—this is the first step toward that gold medal. From this point on, I'll improve every day—one step at a time!"

Determining Your Net Worth

If you were to sell everything you own and pay off all your bills, what you would have left over is called your *net worth*. The formula for net worth looks like this:

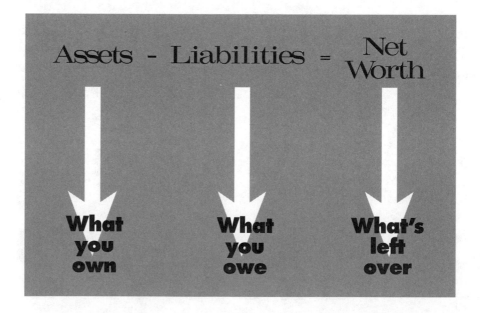

Assets - Liabilities = Net Worth

What you own   **What you owe**   **What's left over**

Your assets may include any, or all, of the following:

- Cash in checking accounts
- Cash in saving accounts
- Money market accounts
- Certificates of deposit
- U.S. Treasury bills
- Common stocks
- Bonds
- Mutual funds
- Limited partnerships
- Investment real estate
- Ownership(s) in private business
- Annuities
- Individual retirement accounts (IRAs)
- 401(k) retirement plans
- Pension/profit-sharing plans
- Keoghs, SEPs
- Cash value of life insurance
- Home (current value)
- Vacation property
- Automobile(s)
- Boat(s)
- Home furnishings
- Collectibles/art/antiques
- Jewelry

Here are some examples of liabilities:

- Credit card balances
- Charge account balances
- Mortgage on personal home
- Mortgage on vacation property
- Mortgage on investment real estate
- Home equity loan
- Education loan
- Bank loan
- Life insurance loan
- 401(k) loan
- Automobile loan
- Income taxes payable
- Miscellaneous accounts payable

Essentially, your net worth is what you have to work with financially. You can find out your present net worth by completing Warm-Up Exercise #1.

 ADVICE FROM THE COACH: Photocopy the Net Worth Worksheet and other forms in the warm-up exercises. Use a pencil and take your time. Because these forms will help determine your training program to win the financial gold medal, be as accurate as possible.

Warm-up Exercise One

Net Worth Worksheet

ASSETS (WHAT YOU OWN):

Cash in checking accounts	$ _____
Cash in savings accounts	_____
Money market accounts	_____
Certificates of deposit	_____
U.S. Treasury bills	_____
Common stocks	_____
Bonds	_____
Mutual funds	_____
Limited partnerships	_____
Investment real estate	_____
Ownership(s) in private business	_____
Annuities	_____
Individual retirement accounts (IRAs)	_____
401(k) retirement plans	_____
Pension/profit-sharing plans	_____
Keoghs, SEPs	_____
Cash value of life insurance*	_____
Home (current value)	_____

*Only certain life insurance policies have cash value that you can borrow.

Vacation property   _____

Automobile(s)   _____

Boat(s)   _____

Home furnishings   _____

Collectibles/art/antiques   _____

Jewelry   _____

Other: _____

TOTAL ASSETS $ _____

LIABILITIES (WHAT YOU OWE):

Credit card balances $ _____

Charge account balances   _____

Mortgage on personal home   _____

Mortgage on vacation property   _____

Mortgage on investment real estate   _____

Home equity loan   _____

Education loan   _____

Bank loan   _____

Life insurance loan   _____

401(k) loan   _____

Automobile loan   _____

Income taxes payable   _____

Miscellaneous accounts payable   _____

Other:

_____   _____

_____   _____

_____   _____

_____   _____

_____   _____

_____   _____

                    TOTAL LIABILITIES $ _____

Now, using the dollar amounts you filled in for "Total Assets" and "Total Liabilities," complete the following:

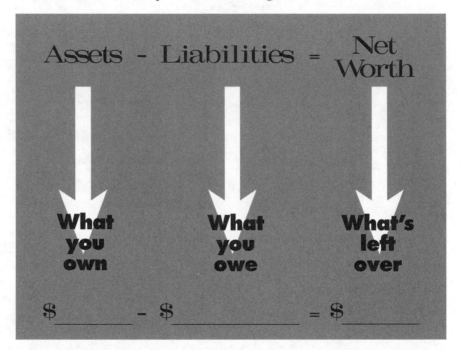

ADVICE FROM THE COACH: Stop right now! Do not panic! Don't get depressed! Remember—this is the BEGINNING of something wonderful. It's just going to take:

- Patience.

- Discipline.

- Persistence.

- A positive attitude.

Preparing an Income Statement

An income statement identifies where your money is coming from. But before you tackle your income statement, identify some of your sources of income. As you read down the list, check off any that apply to you.

- ☐ Salary (before taxes)
- ☐ Bonuses
- ☐ Commissions
- ☐ Child support
- ☐ Alimony
- ☐ Hobby income
- ☐ Self-employment income
- ☐ Trust income
- ☐ Partnership income
- ☐ Public assistance
- ☐ Cash gifts
- ☐ Pension/profit sharing
- ☐ Inheritances
- ☐ Rental property income
- ☐ Stocks, bonds, mutual fund dividends
- ☐ Royalties
- ☐ Annuities, insurance
- ☐ Savings/money market account interest
- ☐ Social Security

☐ Workers' compensation

☐ Insurance proceeds

☐ Proceeds from sale of assets

Now that you've identified your sources of income, you're ready to prepare a monthly income statement.

Warm-up Exercise TWO

Income Statement

WHAT YOU EARN (MONTHLY)

Employment Income:

Salary(ies) $ _____

Commissions/Tips   _____

Bonuses   _____

Hobby/self-employment income   _____

Other: _____   _____

_____   _____

_____   _____

_____   _____

Investment Income:

Dividends $ _____

Interest   _____

Annuities   _____

Rents   _____

Other: _____   _____

_____   _____

_____   _____

_____   _____

Other Income:

Pensions/profit sharing $ _____

Social Security _____

Trust _____

Partnerships _____

Royalties _____

Alimony _____

Child support _____

Workers' compensation _____

Public assistance _____

Other: _____ _____

_____ _____

_____ _____

_____ _____

TOTAL MONTHLY INCOME $ _____

WHAT YOU SPEND (MONTHLY)

Living Expenses:

Rent $ _____

Utilities   _____

Telephone   _____

Home maintenance   _____

Food   _____

Clothing   _____

Health and beauty aids   _____

Household supplies   _____

Child care   _____

Pet needs   _____

Car   _____

Other:_____   _____

_____   _____

_____   _____

Loan Payments:

Car $ _____

Mortgage   _____

Bank loans   _____

Credit cards   _____

Education   _____

Other:_____   _____

_____   _____

_____   _____

Insurance Premiums:

Life $ _____

Health   _____

Disability   _____

Car   _____

Property/casualty   _____

Other:_____   _____

_____   _____

_____   _____

Charitable Contributions:

Church $ _____

Organization   _____

Other:_____   _____

_____   _____

_____   _____

Taxes:

Property $ _____

State/federal income   _____

Other:_____   _____

_____   _____

_____   _____

Other Expenses:

Gifts $ _____

Entertainment   _____

Vacations   _____

Education/tuition   _____

Memberships   _____

Medical/dental   _____

Alimony/child support   _____

Other: _____   _____

_____   _____

_____   _____

_____   _____

_____   _____

_____   _____

_____   _____

_____   _____

_____   _____

                    TOTAL EXPENSES $ _____

To get your monthly picture, complete the following, using the figures you obtained for your total income and total expenses:

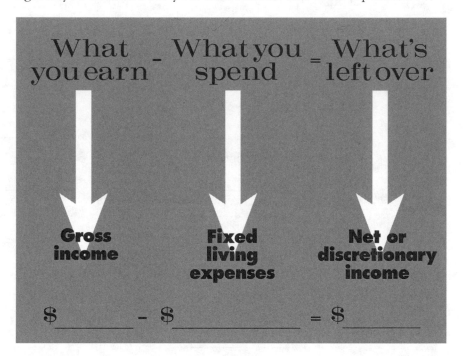

What you earn − What you spend = What's left over

Gross income   Fixed living expenses   Net or discretionary income

$_____ − $_____ = $_____

ADVICE FROM THE COACH: If your net income is in the "minus" category, go directly to Chapter 8 for some good ideas about how to cut down on expenses so that you'll actually *have* income available for saving and investing.

three

The Future:

Are You Ready

to Start

Training?

In order to train for the financial gold medal, you can't settle for being like everyone else—you have to be *better* than average. Most people aren't to begin with, but with careful evaluation, training, and discipline, you *can* be a gold medalist.

In a January 1995 article titled "The Future of Spending," *American Demographics* magazine stated that Americans spend their money as follows:

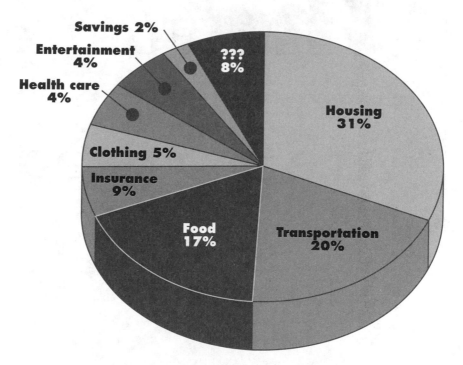

Source: *American Demographics* magazine, © 1995. Used with permission.

Now let's see where *you* are by completing Warm-Up Exercise #3.

Warm-up Exercise Three

Finding Out Where the Money Goes

From your income statement (Chapter 2), fill in the appropriate blanks and then compare them to the Ideal Range numbers.

You'll notice that the numbers at the top end of the Ideal Range don't add up to 100 percent—there may be other expenses that don't fit into these broad categories. And even if you can set up a budget that will make you adhere to the top numbers of each category in the Ideal Range, you'll still have an additional 1 percent of your income for wealth accumulation. Now, you're on the right track!

My Expenses		Ideal Range	
_____ %	Housing	25-29%	Housing
_____ %	Transportation	13-16%	Transportation
_____ %	Food	14-18%	Food
_____ %	Insurance	9-11%	Insurance
_____ %	Clothing	3-5%	Clothing
_____ %	Health care	3-5%	Health care
_____ %	Entertainment	3-5%	Entertainment
_____ %	Savings	8-10%	Savings

Now, if you'd like to see a graphical representation of where you spend your money, draw wedges in the circle below to make a pie chart. Shade in the areas where you aren't in the Ideal Range.

As you study the areas where you're on financially shaky ground, say to yourself, "I must look at the glass as half full, not half empty."

You may be ready to give up, to call it quits, particularly after seeing the results of the warm-up exercises, but *this is not the time to throw in the towel*.

Think about what Thomas Edison once said: "Ninety-nine percent of all failures would have succeeded, if they had kept on trying." So this is the time to get up and try again, and again, and again, and again...and you *will* eventually succeed.

Let's see how you're going to make it happen.

Getting Into Training: Building a Solid Financial Foundation

You've probably read the saying, "People don't plan to fail; they fail to plan." As you begin to train for your gold medal, you will start by developing a plan just as you would if you were building a house. Begin at the bottom and work your way to the top. You can't build the roof and then put in the foundation; you must start with the foundation and work upward. The same principles apply to a financial plan. The foundation for your financial plan consists of two parts:

- Risk management
- Emergency fund

Risk Management

Risk management means asking questions to determine whether you have enough insurance coverage in place to protect yourself in the event of a financial, medical, or natural disaster. The consequences of inadequate insurance can be so devastating that the risk isn't worth it. Without proper insurance protection, you teeter on the edge of disaster and set yourself up for a life of poverty. You cannot build your structure of financial security unless this important foundation piece is in place.

Alternatively, you may have too much insurance, or the wrong kind. Mary is a 44-year-old widow who lost her husband unexpectedly eight months ago. She's done pretty well. She's made no major financial decisions (on advice from her coach) for six months, giving herself that time to grieve, to get use to being alone, and to let the dust settle. She changed to an unlisted phone number, thus eliminating the many annoying sales calls from people who read the obituary columns. She has no children and has done a good job of keeping so busy at work that when she goes home at night, she's too tired to think about anything except going to sleep. Now she's starting to take a look at those financial items that didn't need her immediate attention after her husband's death. Because she's let some time pass, she's now able to look at life and her financial situation with a clear head and a good vision of her future needs.

Mary told her coach: "You know, I've been debating whether I should keep this additional life insurance policy. I already have coverage to pay funeral costs and all bills when I die, and there's no one in my family that I need to leave money to—they're all just fine. Do you think I should drop it?"

The coach replied: "Absolutely! You're well protected with your other coverages, but don't look at it as additional spending money. Set up a good, conservative mutual fund account and have the fund company automatically deduct from your bank account the same amount you're paying for the insurance premiums. That will be the start of building up a nest egg for retirement."

This concept will not cost Mary any additional money. It simply diverts funds she previously used for insurance protection to an account established for her eventual retirement. Find yourself an insurance coach—an agent who can examine your present coverage and see if it's right for you.

The bad news may be that you don't have enough coverage. Remember, the risk for not being adequately covered is too great to take a chance.

The good news, on the other hand, is that you may have too much coverage, or your coverage may be too expensive. You may be able to reduce your insurance costs.

To determine your risk protection needs, ask yourself the questions in Warm-Up Exercise #4.

Warm-up Exercise Four

Determining Your Risk Protection Needs

For each item, answer "yes," "no," or "don't know."

	Yes	No	Don't know
If I work outside the home...			
1. Am I covered at work?	____	____	____
2. Am I covered by my spouse?	____	____	____
3. Am I covered by any medical disability group policies?	____	____	____
4. Do I have dependent children?	____	____	____
5. Is my salary needed for my family to maintain our current standard of living?	____	____	____
6. Do I have dependent parents?	____	____	____
7. Do I intend/need to work until age 65?	____	____	____
8. Do I intend/need to work past age 65?	____	____	____
9. Have I established an emergency fund?	____	____	____

OUACHITA TECHNICAL COLLEGE

	Yes	No	Don't know

If I do not work outside the home...

1. Am I covered by my spouse? ____ ____ ____

2. Am I eligible for any group medical or disability coverage? ____ ____ ____

3. Do I have dependent children? ____ ____ ____

4. Do I have dependent parents? ____ ____ ____

5. Do I have relatives/parents who can afford to care for my children? ____ ____ ____

6. Do I use outside help for housekeeping or child care? ____ ____ ____

Regarding health insurance...

1. Am I covered at work? ____ ____ ____

2. Am I covered by my spouse's policy? ____ ____ ____

3. Am I eligible for any group policies? ____ ____ ____

4. Do I belong to an HMO (health maintenance organization)? ____ ____ ____

5. Do I know the maximum coverage offered by my policy? ____ ____ ____

6. Is my policy guaranteed renewable?* ____ ____ ____

7. Does my policy pay over 80 percent of my health costs? ____ ____ ____

*Guaranteed renewable means that you can renew your policy no matter what the present state of your medical condition is.

	Yes	No	Don't know
Regarding disability insurance...			
1. Am I covered at work?	___	___	___
2. Am I covered by my spouse's policy?	___	___	___
3. Am I eligible for any group policies?	___	___	___
4. Do I know how much my benefit payments will be?	___	___	___
5. Is there a waiting period before my benefit payments begin?	___	___	___
6. Do I know how long my benefit payments will continue?	___	___	___
7. Is my policy restricted to total disability?	___	___	___
8. Does my policy cover accident and illness?	___	___	___

ADVICE FROM THE COACH: It's not unusual for some financial athletes to have answers in the "Don't know" column. This is easy to correct. Read your policy or have your agent review your policy to get the answers to these questions. If you can't find your policy, write a letter to the insurance company and request a duplicate policy. Put this copy in your safe deposit box.

Be sure that the deductibles you establish are no higher than what you can afford to pay in case of loss.

Your liability coverage limits should be the maximum available.

Your life insurance coverage should allow your family to maintain its present standard of living in the event of your death.

So, just how much insurance do I really need?"

It's very simple. Follow these steps:

1. Amount of income my family

   needs to live each month   _____

2. Multiply monthly income needed

   by 12 to get annual income needed   _____   x 12 = _____

You need to buy an insurance policy that, when the proceeds are paid and placed under professional management, will generate the necessary annual income without the principal being touched. Here's an example:

1. Monthly income needed: $3,500

2. Annual income needed: $3,500 x 12 = $42,000

3. Insurance coverage needed: $500,000

The proceeds of the insurance policy ($500,000), when managed professionally to return an annual yield of 8.5 percent, will generate $42,500 annually ($500 more than actually required). What is needed here besides the appropriate coverage is a good money manager (more later on this subject). The $42,000 needed annually doesn't take into consideration that, because of inflation, the dollar may not purchase as much in the future as it does today. But with sound, conservative investing, the reduction of the dollar's purchasing power may be counteracted by the increase of principal under management.

In the late 1700s, Benjamin Franklin set up a two-hundred-year trust to be professionally managed for the city of Boston, and the resulting funds generated for the city have surpassed the 8.5 percent figure used in the previous example.

ADVICE FROM THE COACH: Shop around for your insurance! Talk to several companies and several agents. Consider buying your insurance from a professional who represents several different companies so that you have a variety of products, services, *and* rates to choose from. There are as many different kinds of insurance policies as there are automobiles, so take a look around and talk to several people in the business until you find the agent who will do the best job for you.

Insurance may seem like a costly nuisance, a pain in the neck, but you will never meet a woman or man who complained that his or her deceased spouse had purchased too much insurance. You will never meet victims of a hurricane, earthquake, flood, or fire who ever thought they carried too much insurance.

Emergency Fund

You'll notice that when you start to build your financial house, insurance (risk management) is the foundation, but there's another crucial part of this important base:

The crucial part is the stairs—establishing an emergency fund. If you don't put in these stairs, you're not going anywhere. An emergency fund is a special account that is set aside and never touched unless an emergency arises in the family. There are two kinds of emergency funds:

- **Bill-paying emergency fund**

  This fund holds enough money to pay all your bills for the next three to six months if your income suddenly stops. Disability payments and Social Security checks take an average of three to six months to start arriving after a claim is filed. This type of emergency fund is a *must* for all families. Set up this fund in a separate savings account, preferably with two names on it, so that if one partner is severely injured or disabled, the other trusted partner has access to pay the bills.

- **Replacement fund**

  This fund is set up to cover the replacement cost of large items your family needs. We're not talking VCRs and stereos here—although some people *don't* think they can do without them, these items really aren't crucial for comfort and survival.

Use the following worksheets to determine how much it would cost to replace some items you own—and how much money you should set aside in case of an emergency. It will also help you determine how much you need to set aside each month to meet this type of emergency.

Warm-up Exercise Five

Replacement Fund for Appliances

Appliances	Average Life	Replacement Cost	Life Left in Present Item	Need to Save Per Month
Air Conditioner				
Furnace				
Refrigerator				
Stove				
Water Heater				
Washer				
Dryer				
Other:				

Warm-up Exercise Six

Replacement Fund for Home Maintenance

Home Maintenance	Average Life	Replacement Cost	Life Left in Present Item	Need to Save Per Month
Roof				
Plumbing				
Exterior/Siding				
Floor Coverings				
Electrical				
Landscaping				
Wall Coverings				
Other:				

Example:

Appliances	Average Life	Replacement Cost	Life Left in Present Item	Need to Save Per Month
Air Conditioner	12 years	$1,600	11 years	$12.00
Furnace				

To make sure that you save enough for your emergency funds, contribute a set amount each month and treat it as a fixed expense on your income statement.

Investment Management

Now that you have the foundation of your financial security plan in place, it's time to start working on the next level of your financial house, the frame: investment management.

But where do you begin? What materials do you use? Actually there are a number of investments you can choose from, including the following:

- Mutual funds

- Money market funds

- Annuities

- Unit investment trusts

- Stocks

- Options

- Bonds

- Real estate

- Commodities

Types of Investments

You can simplify your selection when you realize that all investments fall into one of four categories:

1. Cash and Cash Equivalents.

Cash includes paper currency, coins, money orders, checks, and bank balances. Cash equivalents are instruments or investments of such high liquidity and safety that they are virtually as good as cash. Examples would include money market funds and treasury bills.

- **Money market funds.** These act like a savings account, but you can write checks from the funds in the account.

- **Certificates of deposit.** CDs require you to lock in an interest rate for a specified period of time. If you take out the money before the interest rate period is completed, you'll pay a substantial penalty and lose any interest the CD may have earned in the future. CDs are insured by the FDIC (Federal Deposit Insurance Corporation) up to $100,000.

- **Treasury bills.** Sold by the U.S. government, these bills are sort of a government "IOU." They offer a set interest rate for a fixed period.

2. Real Estate.

Real estate includes a piece of land and all the physical property related to it, including houses, fences, landscaping, and all rights to the air above and earth below the property.

- **Your home.** This is usually your single largest investment. Depending on where you live and the real estate values there, this investment can prove to be excellent or simply afford you a place to live. There may come a time when the interest you pay on your mortgage will no longer be deductible from your income tax. This is the case in Canada and several other countries, so keep this prospect in mind when considering an investment of this type.

- **Investment real estate.** If you purchase rental property or land that is earmarked for development, realize that this type of investment is not easily turned into cash. Before you buy, consider the fate of Albert Lowery, who came to fame with his 1977 book, *How You Can Become Financially Independent by Investing in Real Estate*. By 1979, the book was a best-seller, and people were paying $495 to attend his weekend seminars. Mr. Lowery was grossing $100,000 to $200,000 per weekend in large metropolitan areas. However, real estate took a nosedive in the mid-1980s, and the real world set in. The concept of buying real estate with "no money down" didn't work with falling real estate prices, and Mr. Lowery declared bankruptcy in 1987, preceded and followed by many of his former students who thought they were going to get rich quickly.

Real estate can be an excellent investment, but you must do your homework and know exactly what you're getting into. Don't just get a second opinion—get a third, a fourth, and a fifth one before investing this way.

3. **Stocks.** Stocks are shares offered for sale by organizations. You can buy individual stocks through a brokerage firm or a portfolio of stocks by investing in a mutual fund. "Blue chip" stocks are issued by large, financially stable companies such as Microsoft, General Motors, IBM, and Merrill Lynch. Smaller company stocks may show greater volatility (increases and decreases of the price of the share), but they have a higher growth potential.

4. **Bonds.** The government (federal, state, local) and corporations both issue bonds to raise capital for their organizations. As an example, a county may put forth a bond issue to raise money to build a new library, airport, or something else in that county. You lend them money by buying bonds, and they give you an IOU that promises to pay you back in a certain time frame with interest. There are three basic types of bonds:

   - **U.S. government bonds.** These are relatively safe and offer predictable income.

   - **Municipal bonds.** Issued by state and local governments, these bonds offer current income exempt from federal taxes. Such investments are suitable for retired persons who need a stream of income but also desire to reduce their income taxes.

   - **Corporate bonds.** These are issued by corporations to raise capital for such goals as expansion, product development, and research, or simply to stay in business.

At this point, you're probably saying to yourself: "HELP! What do I do now? There are too many choices! Which of these is right for me?"

ADVICE FROM THE COACH: If you want to invest to get rich overnight, this coach will ask you to get off the team and leave training camp immediately!

Risk Tolerance

First you must know your *risk tolerance.* In other words, you must ask yourself, "If I put my money into this investment, will I be able to sleep at night?" If the answer is "no," don't do it. That investment isn't suitable for you.

How do you determine your risk (investment) tolerance? Complete Warm-Up Exercise #7.

Warm-up Exercise Seven

Determining Your Risk Tolerance

1. You're on a television game show, and you've won $500. You are given three choices. Which one do you choose?

    A. Take the money and run.

    B. Compete with another person to win $1,000. If you don't win, you lose $250.

    C. Compete with ten people to win $100,000. If you don't win, you lose the $500.

2. You're driving your year-old car. It's raining heavily and visibility is poor. You aren't familiar with this particular highway. Up ahead the road is completely covered with water. What do you do?

    A. Speed up, hoping the increase in speed will get you through the water.

    B. Turn around, drive to the nearest town, and inquire about road conditions.

    C. Slow down and get ready to put the car in reverse if the water gets too deep.

3. You scratch off a lottery ticket. It gives you the following three options. Which one do you choose?

   A. Send the ticket in by registered mail and receive a check for $100.

   B. Go on TV and spin "The Big Wheel" with the possibility of winning everything or nothing.

   C. Redeem the ticket for 100 new lottery tickets.

4. Your favorite game to play is:

   A. Poker.

   B. Craps.

   C. Old Maid.

5. You are an average skier. You:

   A. Are content with your level of ability and ski on the slopes suited for you.

   B. Take ski lessons with the goal of improving in order to confidently tackle the more difficult ski runs.

   C. Say "What the heck" and try the expert slopes anyway.

6. You have worked long and hard for your income. You have accumulated a small nest egg. You get a "very hot" tip about an emerging growth company stock from your next door neighbor who is a stock broker. You:

   A. Visit the library and try to secure financials and information about the company.

   B. Leave the money in your savings account.

   C. Allow the neighbor broker to invest the money for you in the stock.

7. When you invest your savings, you always:

   A. Do what a financial advisor tells you, saying, "Okay, if that's what you think I should do."

   B. Tell the advisor that this investment does not fit within your comfort level.

   C. Secure as much information as you can from the advisor, saying, "I need to examine this more closely."

8. Your perception of a risky investment is:

   A. A growth and income stock mutual fund.

   B. A limited partnership of coin-operated wedding chapels in Las Vegas.

   C. A certificate of deposit.

9. You receive a letter in the mail saying that you have a one-in-five chance to win $5,000. The letter asks for a $59.95 entry and processing fee. You:

   A. Throw the letter in the trash.

   B. Call the Better Business Bureau to see if the company is legitimate.

   C. Send the letter back with a check for $59.95.

10. You are a first-time visitor to a gambling casino. You:

   A. Play craps.

   B. Play the slot machines.

   C. Just watch.

11. In the first 20 minutes at a gambling casino, you gamble $5 and win $300. You feel like you're on a lucky streak. You:

   A. Continue to play, hoping to win more.

   B. Agree to leave if you lose $100 of your winnings.

   C. Take your winnings and leave.

12. You dream of:

   A. Building wealth through a systematic investment plan over the next twenty years.

   B. Making a million on the stock market.

   C. Putting all your savings under the mattress for the next twenty years.

13. You attend multilevel marketing seminars. You:

   A. Listen, but take no action.

   B. Run to the back of the room to sign up.

   C. Don't go to these seminars.

14. You go to the horse races. You bet on:

   A. The longshot at 24-1 odds.

   B. The 2-1 favorite.

   C. An 8-1 horse ridden by a winning jockey.

15. When the balances on your credit cards are climbing, you:

   A. Cut up the cards.

   B. Use them only for extreme situations.

   C. Continue to use them and apply for another card.

Total your score:

Question		Points
1.	A	1
	B	2
	C	3
2.	A	3
	B	1
	C	2
3.	A	1
	B	3
	C	2
4.	A	2
	B	3
	C	1
5.	A	1
	B	2
	C	3
6.	A	2
	B	1
	C	3
7.	A	3
	B	1
	C	2
8.	A	2
	B	3
	C	1

Question		Points
9.	A	1
	B	2
	C	3
10.	A	3
	B	2
	C	1
11.	A	3
	B	2
	C	1
12.	A	1
	B	2
	C	3
13.	A	2
	B	3
	C	1
14.	A	3
	B	1
	C	2
15.	A	1
	B	2
	C	3

If you scored:

15-24. You are a very cautious person with a fairly low risk tolerance. You will sleep better with stable, conservative, slow but steady growth types of investments such as annuities, bonds, certificates of deposit, and treasury bills.

25-36. You are a moderate risk-taker, willing to take a chance but only after thoroughly examining the investment vehicle. You will probably have some money in safe investments but also put the earnings in a few aggressive types of stock and international mutual funds. You may try your hand at the stock market, pulling back if you lose more than a predetermined amount of money.

37-45. Whoa, Nelly! You are comfortable taking a lot of risk and will invest in individual stocks and aggressive mutual funds. Your philosophy is, "If I don't play, I can't win!"

Investment Pyramids

Almost everyone involved in financial planning today is familiar with the *investment pyramid*, a great way to visualize whether your investment planning is properly positioned. Study the coach's investment pyramid below, and then fill in the blank pyramid with your own investments to see how well you're doing. When planning your future, you should fill in the base first, and then work your way to the top.

Coach's Investment Pyramid

Your Investment Pyramid

Base Section

- Emergency fund
- Insurance protection
- Purchase of home
- Wills
- Savings, money market fund accounts
- Annuities

Safety Section

- Stable, conservative investments
- Bonds, bond mutual funds
- Blue chip stock mutual funds
- Government securities

Growth Section

- Growth stocks or stock mutual funds
- Investment real estate
- Capital appreciation mutual funds
- Utilities mutual funds

Risk Section (the smallest part of your investment program)

- Options
- Commodities
- Junk (lower-graded) bonds
- Precious metals
- Oil and gas

The above-listed investments certainly don't offer a complete picture. But if an advisor is trying to sell you an investment, ask him or her which category the investment falls under and then see if it's suitable for your risk tolerance level. Don't let a promised high return tempt you to take a risk that will make you feel uncomfortable. Remember, you have to be able to sleep at night. If it sounds too good to be true, it probably is!

ADVICE FROM THE COACH: If you are new to investing, the most comfortable and successful method can be using mutual funds. Each is comprised of as many as 150 different stock and bond issues, depending on the objective of the fund. Funds are a great way to diversify your money rather than investing in a single stock or bond. Choose one that is more than ten to fifteen years old. Mutual funds are riding high these days, and all sorts of smaller companies are part of the "Let's start a mutual fund and make a killing!" syndrome. However, when and if funds go down (everything is cyclical), the smaller companies fold up their tents and silently steal away. Several mutual fund companies have gone through the 1929 stock market crash in addition to the dramatic downturn of 1987, and they are doing a good job and staying healthy financially. Read Chapter 4 for more details.

Tax Planning

Now that the frame (investment planning) of your financial house is up, the next step is the roof—a shelter for your income.

Nobody likes to pay taxes, but we all must pay our fair share in order to have good highways, safe communities, and well-educated children. But you certainly don't need to pay *more* than your fair share. The following pages offer ways to soften the tax blow.

Invest Tax Free

You can invest in municipal bonds or municipal bond mutual funds. By doing this, you decrease your tax burden because these investments yield interest that is free from federal taxation.

Shifting or Gifting

You can reduce the value of your estate by shifting or gifting assets to children or grandchildren. Couples can pass a sizable amount of their estate to beneficiaries (check with a financial advisor for current limits) without them having to pay federal inheritance taxes. Everything over the limits is taxable—why not reduce that amount by making gifts of cash to children or grandchildren? This is a good idea—and not just from the tax angle. While you're alive, you get to see a grandchild earn a college degree (thanks to you!), or a son or daughter buy a new home (again due to your generosity). You're around to share the pleasure you give to your family members.

Postponing

Your third choice is to postpone or defer taxes by taking advantage of investment programs such as individual retirement accounts (IRAs) or the many other plans that provide this opportunity. You don't pay any taxes on these assets until you withdraw the money at retirement time. Descriptions of your retirement plan options follow:

- **Individual retirement account.** An IRA is a personal retirement fund for people who have earned income from wages, salary, self-employment income, professional fees, bonuses, tips, and so forth. Currently, contributions are limited to $2,000 or 100 percent of your earned income, whichever is less. The contribution by one-income couples can total $2,250 as long as no more than $2,000 is allocated to either spouse.

Portions of an IRA may be tax deductible, depending on whether you are covered by any other type of retirement plan. Any financial advisor will know the current limitations.

Once your money is in the plan, it's allowed to grow on a tax-deferred basis until you withdraw it. You can begin to withdraw without penalty beginning at age 59 1/2, and you must start withdrawing at age 70 1/2. If you must withdraw before age 59 1/2, the money withdrawn is subject to taxes as well as a hefty penalty for early withdrawal. And, of course, the withdrawn money can no longer grow on a tax-deferred basis.

- **Keogh.** A Keogh plan allows for contributions far in excess of $2,000 a year. A Keogh was designed for those who are self-employed and not incorporated. A person can put away 20 percent of self-employment income up to a maximum of $30,000 a year.

- **SEP-IRA.** You can save the lesser of 13.04 percent of self-employment income up to a maximum of $22,500 per year. These contributions are tax deductible from taxable income, and the money grows tax-deferred until withdrawal.

- **401(k).** 401(k) plans are a very attractive choice for many people. These retirement plans are set up by employers as a benefit to employees. Money is taken out of an employee's salary, invested in the 401(k) plan, and then not taxed until it is withdrawn. 401(k) plans are excellent "forced savings" plans. What you don't have in your hand, you're not going to spend. Since employers can match your contributions, what you invest can possibly be doubled, depending on the parameters set by the corporation. As a rule, you cannot receive the corporation's contributions until you are "vested" (stay with the company for a predetermined number of years), but there are borrowing privileges under certain circumstances such as financial hardship.

- **403(b).** 403(b) plans are available through nonprofit organizations. They allow investors to borrow against the fund balance without penalty. Remember, it's not a good idea to raid your retirement savings account.

ADVICE FROM THE COACH: Many organizations allow employees to determine the percentage to be deducted from their salary. *Maximize it!* What you don't see, you're not going to spend. You may groan the first time the larger amount is deducted, but you will get used to the smaller paycheck quickly. And given the many retirement plans available, you will have a large variety of investment vehicles to choose from.

The preceding paragraphs described just a few of the methods available for accumulating income and deferring taxes on the compounded amount until retirement. *Do your homework!* Meet with your personnel department and work or check with a qualified financial advisor—not a person whose only solution to your challenge is to sell you an insurance-based product.

Retirement and Estate Planning

Dennis R. Deaton, in *Money: An Owner's Manual*, shared sobering statistics from the 1989 U.S. Department of Commerce Income and Poverty Report. For every 100 U.S. citizens born in 1923, the groups showed the following profile when the members reached retirement age (65):

29   Deceased

14   Annual income under $5,000

51   Incomes of $5,000 to $25,000

5   Annual income of $25,000 to $50,000

1   Annual income over $50,000

Deaton also conveyed the Social Security Administration's acknowledgment that almost 90 percent of the people in this country enter retirement with less than $500 in their bank books.

The final phase of your financial house building is putting in the windows so that you can see your life ahead as one that is happy and comfortable:

Let's talk about the bad news first:

Because the dollar you earn today won't buy as much in the future, the dollars you put aside for retirement need to grow as much as possible so that at retirement you can at least maintain the same standard of living. Unfortunately, that's not the case for many people. According to David Chilton, in *The Wealthy Barber*, perhaps well over 50 percent of retired people need some form of government assistance to survive.

Your goal should be to live comfortably at retirement without having to depend on Social Security to help pay the bills. It seems unclear just how long Social Security and other government assistance programs will exist, so you need to plan for financial independence as if they've *never* existed.

Well then, just how much does a person need to put aside today to live comfortably at retirement? To maintain your current standard of living, the experts say you'll need 75 to 80 percent of your current income after retirement. To see some real figures, complete Warm-Up Exercise #8.

Eight

Retirement Income Worksheet

Monthly Expense Needs

Fill out this section to determine your monthly expense needs.

Current age _____   Proposed Retirement Age _____

Monthly Expense Needs	Today	At Retirement (in today's dollars)
Rent/mortgage	_____	_____
Food	_____	_____
Clothing	_____	_____
Laundry/cleaning	_____	_____
Utilities	_____	_____
Household supplies	_____	_____
Transportation	_____	_____
Health/beauty aids	_____	_____
Medical/dental	_____	_____
Insurance	_____	_____
Church/charity	_____	_____
Entertainment	_____	_____
Property taxes	_____	_____
Hobbies	_____	_____
Travel	_____	_____

Gifts _____ _____

Club dues _____ _____

Other: _____ _____

_____ _____ _____

_____ _____ _____

_____ _____ _____

_____ _____ _____

_____ _____ _____

_____ _____ _____

_____ _____ _____

_____ _____ _____

**Total Monthly
Estimated Expenses** _____ _____

Income

Now estimate your income. Note the example in the first column.

	Example	You
1. Your estimated annual retirement income from Social Security payments, pensions, IRAs, investments, etc.	$30,000	
2. Your estimated annual expenses (monthly expenses x 12)	$75,000	
3. Subtract line 2 from line 1 to determine the amount needed to live as you are today	($45,000)	
4. Number of years you want retirement to cover	25	
5. Additional retirement funds needed	$125,000	
6. Months to retirement (years x 12)	60	
7. Amount needed to save each month to reach retirement goal	$18,750	

This illustration isn't meant to frighten you (the age of the person in the example is 60), but to point out that the earlier you start to plan for retirement, the easier it is to accomplish. Get started *now!*

Four

Getting

the Picture

of Mutual

Funds

There are a great many different mutual fund companies, and each has a "family" of funds from which you can choose. It's always wise to invest with a company that's been around for at least a decade or more and has a variety of funds to meet almost every investment objective available. The reason for investing with a family is when the occasion calls for you to change your investment objective, you can move from one fund to another within the family without incurring another sales charge.

Types of Mutual Funds

Depending on the length of your goal and your investment objective, here is a sampling of the kinds of mutual funds you can choose from.

Aggressive Growth Funds

These funds seek maximum capital gains as the main investment objective. Rarely is a significant level of income produced, and active investment in speculative stocks is the norm. This type of fund suits long-term "buy and hold" investing. Usually the portfolio will be fully committed to stocks, which can be the most volatile, but also the most rewarding, investment avenue over a period of time. These funds have a high reward potential, but they are the most unpredictable of all the funds.

Growth Funds

The primary objective here is long-term growth, but the process involves less speculative investments. The focus is on increasing the value of the investments in the fund rather than on generating income from the flow of dividends. The manager will usually select well-established, growth-oriented companies to produce a more stable atmosphere than aggressive growth funds.

Specialty Funds

The investment issues in a specialty fund may concentrate on a particular industry, geographic location, or company type. Examples of specialty funds include precious metals funds, international funds, and global funds.

Growth/Income Funds

These funds attempt to combine long-term capital growth with a steady stream of current income, usually in the form of stock dividends but possibly also from bond or money market interest. A fund of this type might invest in dividend-paying common stocks of larger, established companies, public utility common stocks, corporate convertible bonds, and convertible preferred stocks as well.

Balanced Funds

The investment objective of balanced funds has three parts: to preserve the investor's initially invested principal, to pay current income, and to achieve moderate long-term growth of both invested principal and income. The portfolio will be a diversified mix of both common and preferred stocks as well as bonds and money market instruments.

Option Income Funds

These funds are invested in dividend-paying common stocks on which call options are traded on securities exchanges. Their current return consists of dividends, premiums from writing options, and the results of other options-related transactions.

Equity Income Funds

The objective of these funds is to seek a current level of high-paying income for the investors. The manager will seek securities that pay high current income, derived mainly from dividends. Your portfolio will consist of companies that have good dividend-paying records, as well as bonds and money market investments.

Corporate Bond Funds

The portfolio here is primarily invested in bonds or debt instruments by sound, well-managed companies. The goal of the fund is to seek a high level of income along with stability of principal. Capital growth is a minor consideration. This type of fund may be attractive to people who have retired and seek the income to add to their retirement while preserving the principal.

Municipal Bond Funds

The income that municipal bond funds provide is free of federal taxes and is achieved by investing in bonds issued by local governments such as cities and states. The invested money goes toward projects such as the construction of highways, schools, and libraries. There are also single-state municipal bond funds that invest only in the issues of one state. The investors residing in that state will receive income that is both federal and state tax free. In some cases, the income also may be free of local tax.

U.S. Government Securities Funds

These funds invest in a variety of government securities, including U.S. Treasury bonds, federally guaranteed mortgage-backed securities, and other government notes. A high level of current income and a higher degree of safety would be the objective of investing in this type of fund.

GNMA or Ginnie Mae Funds

The objective of these funds is to combine a higher degree of safety with attractive levels of current income by investing in mortgage securities pooled by the Government National Mortgage Association and backed by the U.S. government. The government backs the principal and interest on the GNMA securities themselves, not the value of the funds' shares. The value of the shares will fluctuate according to the level of interest rates and other market conditions.

Money Market Mutual Funds

The portfolio of the money market fund will typically include Treasury bills, certificates of deposit of large banks, and commercial paper. These funds present a good place to put surplus cash for the short term because money market funds have check-writing privileges (many with a $100 to $500 minimum) and earn slightly better interest than a regular checking or savings account. It's always a good idea to open a money market fund along with any other mutual fund in the same family because if you need quick cash, you can liquidate shares of your regular fund, have the money transferred to the money market fund (at no charge), and simply write a check for the amount you need.

Tax-Exempt Money Market Funds

These funds are basically the same as a standard money market fund, except the manager invests exclusively in securities issued by city and/or state governments that are either short term in nature or purchased close to their maturity. The income is free of federal taxation, and many such funds permit you to write checks for large expenditures.

So there are the highlights of just a few of the many kinds of funds available. You should first determine your risk tolerance, then decide the length of time you wish to invest your money, and then work with a financial coach to choose the fund that can help you meet your objectives. Many objectives have different time horizons, so knowing the length of time is crucial in determining which fund will meet your needs. Any good financial coach will help you make the choice and take the time to explain why the fund will be the right one for you.

No Load Funds—Load Funds—12b(1) Funds—Which Is Best?

The answer is "none." The *real* answer is "The fund that meets your specific needs and does the best job for you."

There actually is no such thing as a "no-load" fund. These funds do not charge you a sales commission when you purchase shares, but you will pay an annual maintenance fee that in some cases can exceed the original purchase charge. If the fund is a no-load fund, then you should ask, "How much is the annual maintenance fee?" Many load funds have wonderful performance records and should be looked at closely. It would be better to pay a sales commission or up-front purchase charge on a fund that does well than no up-front charges on a no-load fund that does poorly.

Many no-load funds also don't communicate very often to let you know how they are doing. And you will never get advice from a coach on whether to sell or purchase more shares. With a no-load fund, you are basically doing business with your mailbox.

12b(1) funds also can be very attractive. You invest initially without paying a sales charge, and then there's a descending sales charge that you pay only if you withdraw the funds from the account. If you leave the money in for a period of four or five years (each fund may be different), then the sales charge will disappear at that point. This is good for the fund because it encourages you to leave your money in so that the manager can do something advantageous with it. It's very difficult for a portfolio manager to properly manage a mutual fund if money is constantly being added and withdrawn by investors who don't understand that the best investment method is to buy and hold. The longer the money stays in the fund, the better the manager will be able to work with the funds to meet the portfolio's objective.

Fee Versus Commission— What Is the Best Way to Pay a Financial Coach?

There are three ways a financial coach may earn money:

1. Commissions from the sale of investment and insurance products that you purchase

2. Fees from preparing a financial plan for you (but you still have to purchase the recommended products to put your plan into action)

3. Fees and commissions (you may pay a charge for the financial plan in addition to the products to put the plan in action)

Any of these methods is fine, but you have to have confidence in the financial coach's ability to do what you want to accomplish. Do you trust this person? Does he or she have your best interest at heart? Does he or she take the time to explain any charges or fees associated with the plan or investments? The point here is that if the coach develops a good plan and implements the correct products to make the plan work, you will be in a good financial place, and the coach will have correctly earned his or her fees or commissions. In other words, a coach who does a great job for you is entitled to be fairly compensated for his or her good advice and proper placement of your funds.

Look Out for the
Scam Artists

Some time ago, a client visited a financial planner and said: "How do I file a complaint with the Securities and Exchange Commission? I just lost $50,000 in a deal. And I would like you to do a financial plan for me."

The planner explained that she would work with the client to fill out a preliminary confidential questionnaire and then take him to an attorney nearby who was a specialist in investment fraud cases. Just before introducing him to the attorney, the planner suggested that the client return to her office in three weeks so she could present an initial plan for his review.

Three weeks later, during his second visit with the planner, the client said, "Oh, by the way, I dropped the lawsuit." The planner responded, "You did? You lost a lot of money!" To which the client replied, "Yes, well, when I told them what I was doing, they said that if I continued to do it, I couldn't get in on their next deal!"

A very true and very sad story. There are many scam artists waiting for you to hand over your money.

You must do your homework. Be skeptical of deals offering high returns and quick increases in the value of your investment. If the investment program hasn't been cleared by the National Association of Securities Dealers, walk away. Even if it has, it may not be safe. The NASD does not approve a deal—they only make sure that no fraudulent claims are made in the prospectus and marketing information. You are much better off developing a relationship with a financial coach who can do the research for you and know the questions to ask to reveal a "funny money" deal. No ethical financial coach will touch one—and you shouldn't either.

Many scam artists are superb salespeople—they have to be in order to convince you to abandon your instincts and common sense and get into their program. Never hand money over before reading all the literature at home. Don't let anyone get you to invest on the spot. That effort alone should be a big warning signal for you. High pressure sales can mean that they plan to take your money and never see you again. A good financial coach will have an ongoing relationship with you and will continually let you know the details about the successes or problems with any financial program. He or she will not hesitate to deliver bad news, knowing that honesty is essential in developing a good working financial partnership.

How to Read an Investment Prospectus

The Securities and Exchange Commission places stringent requirements on what investment companies must tell potential investors. It's not unusual for a company to rewrite a prospectus many times before it satisfies the SEC's requirements—the commission is just trying to protect you, the investor. Any company that omits information or misstates facts will suffer severe penalties as determined by the SEC; therefore, the language in a prospectus tends to be very technical in order to comply with SEC regulations. Don't even *think* of investing in a program that doesn't have a prospectus to give to investors.

Here's how to use a prospectus:

- Look for the minimum investment figure. Most investment programs stipulate a minimum amount in order to open an account. If the minimum is too high for you, there's no use reading any further.

- Read the statement of investment objectives. There are twenty-one different investment objectives as defined by the Investment Company Institute. First determine what your investment goals are, and then see if the investment objectives stated in the prospectus match them.

- Take a look at the fee table (it's usually near the front). There's no free lunch—even no-load funds have fees. Are there charges for "transactions" (moving money in and out of the fund)? Are there sales charges deducted on any dividends that you reinvest into the same fund? Is there a "contingent deferred sales charge" (sales charge if you cash in your shares of the fund)?

- What class are the shares? This can be confusing. Fund companies may offer several "classes" of funds. As an example:

  Class A. You pay a front-end sales charge when you buy shares of the fund.

  Class B. You pay a deferred sales (back-end) charge coupled with *annual* 12b–1 fees instead of a front-end charge. Typically, the longer shares are held, the lower the charge, with no charge imposed if shares are held more than four or five years.

- Is there a "redemption fee"? Do you get charged for cashing in your shares?

- Is there an "exchange fee"? Some companies will charge you for exchanging all or part of your investment from one fund to another within the same family.

- Look at the "financial highlights" table. This will show you how the fund is doing. You can see what your money would have earned in dividends and capital gains distributions on one share for each year. You will be able to see the increase or decrease in the value of that share.

- Check out the performance of the fund. The SEC requires funds to use certain formulas to determine performance. You can use this information to compare funds with similar objectives. You cannot compare the performance of an aggressive growth fund with a bond fund, for instance—their objectives are entirely different. You must compare apples to apples.

A PARTIAL MUTUAL FUND PORTFOLIO

SHARES	COMMON STOCKS—CONTINUED	MARKET VALUE
	Food & Beverages (7.4%)	
280,000	CPC International Inc. (Major food distribution company)	$13,510,000
460,000	The Coca-Cola Company (World-wide leader in soft drinks)	19,147,500
390,000	Kellog Company (World's premier marketer of cereals)	19,646,250
		52,303,750
	Insurance (3.0%)	
310,000	Marsh & McLennan Companies, Inc. (Largest international insurance broker)	26,195,000

- Take a look at the investment's portfolio. What types of securities (stocks, bonds, or money markets) does this fund purchase to reach its investment goals? Look for any investment restrictions. If you are opposed to tobacco or alcohol, for example, you would check the portfolio to see if shares of tobacco or alcohol companies are purchased. If you are super conservative, you probably don't want to invest in a fund that allows commodities or options trading.

- Every fund will state the investment risks that might be associated with it. This will help you determine if the level of risk is comfortable. All investments have risk—some, in order to meet the fund's investment objective, will be allowed to take more risk.

- What is the turnover rate of the portfolio? In other words, how often do they buy and sell shares in the portfolio? Many funds will have more than a hundred different types of stocks and bonds within the portfolio. If forty of these are traded within a year, the turnover rate would be 40 percent. This may increase the expenses of the portfolio and could reduce the return to investors.

- Does the fund allow for the following?

    a. Telephone redemption or exchange (you can cash in or move your dollars to another fund by telephone)

    b. Wire transfer (you can redeem shares and have the funds transferred to your bank account within twenty-four hours)

    c. Account reports (monthly or whenever a transaction is made)

    d. Automatic bank withdrawal accounts (dollar cost averaging for automatic monthly investing)

    e. Customer service (you can get any question answered promptly in a format that is friendly and understandable)

five

Time-Tested Strategies That Yield Pure Gold

This chapter includes a variety of suggestions, practical tips, and time-tested ideas for maintaining your direction along the road to financial success.

Pay Yourself First

This concept can't be stressed strongly enough! Although you should put your name at the head of your list of creditors, here's what everyone *usually* does: You pay the mortgage or rent, the car payment, the telephone, the utilities, the insurance, the cable service, the credit cards—VISA, MasterCard, American Express, etc., etc., etc. And guess what? There's barely enough to cover all those bills. In fact, some months you only can pay the minimum due on the credit cards. Of course, there's also nothing left to invest. Do not pass "Go," do not collect $200; go directly to jail! This is the *wrong* way to do it!

Instead, *pay yourself first*. That is, first put $25, or $50, or $100, into that growth mutual fund; *then* write the check for the mortgage, the car, the gas, the telephone, and so forth.

Helen Davis kept telling her financial coach that she had no funds available at the end of the month for investment. Her money ran out before her month did. Her coach suggested this experiment: For one month, the coach would purchase Helen's food for her. Helen agreed. Each week she gave her coach the list of her needs. The coach bought the food and overcharged Helen for the items. The coach very carefully kept accurate records of each overcharge and kept the extra cash locked away. At the end of the month, she met with Helen and spread out over $100 on the desk. Helen asked, "Where did that come from?" The coach replied: "It's yours. I overcharged you and kept the overcharged amount for you to prove that you *do* have money for investment. You just need to pay yourself first." Helen was overwhelmed.

There are two excellent books that promote this theory. Both *The Richest Man in Babylon* by George S. Clason and *The Instant Millionaire* by Mark Fisher emphasize the importance of paying yourself first. Follow the advice of these two books and you'll have funds available to achieve your dreams and goals. All it takes is knowledge and planning. The more you learn, the more you will earn.

Dollar Cost Averaging

Dollar cost averaging (DCA) offers one of the most effective methods of investment accumulation and management ever created. It can operate as a combination of the following strategies:

- Pay yourself first.
- Buy and hold.
- Realize the magic of compound interest.
- Believe that time is money.

Very possibly the children of the '90s won't be able to count on Social Security for retirement. Given this, it's unfortunate that investment concepts aren't taught in high school when future earners are on the brink of their first paycheck.

Dollar cost averaging means that you invest a sum of money each month into an investment where DCA is permitted. The money goes in—without fail. In practically all cases, the money is automatically deducted from your bank account (with your consent) by a mutual fund company. Let's see what happens:

You agree to invest $100 per month in a growth stock mutual fund. You are twenty-five years of age and you would like to build a nest egg so that you can retire at age fifty-five.

Month 1. During this first month, $100 is transferred from your bank account to the mutual fund company to be invested in a capital appreciation (growth) fund. The price of the fund share at the time of transfer was $10. Your $100 bought ten shares.

Dollars Invested	Price per Share	Number of Shares Purchased
$100	$10	10

Month 2. The second month the price per share dropped dramatically (*not* a common occurrence) to $5, but your $100 still goes in.

Dollars Invested	Price per Share	Number of Shares Purchased
$100	$5	20

The bad news is that the price of the share went down, but the good news is that your $100 bought twenty shares—twice as many as the month before.

Month 3. The third month the price per share goes up to $10 again, and your third $100 is invested:

Dollars Invested	Price per Share	Number of Shares Purchased
$100	$10	10

By the end of Month 3, you own forty shares. If the price of the share had remained constant, your $100 would have purchased only ten shares per month, and the total number of shares that you would now own would be thirty, not forty as in the example above.

The lesson you want to learn here is that even if the price per share goes down, you are buying a greater number of shares. So the declining price of the share is *not* bad news if you can be patient and only sell when the price of the shares is higher than what you paid for them. This is called "taking your profits."

The preceding shows why the wisest, most cautious investors will *buy and hold* their shares for long periods of time, never looking at the daily published price per share. If an investor is confident in the company and the fund manager, he or she will be patient and keep the monthly payments going in to the mutual fund without fail.

Yes, there may be a time or two when the fund's performance is not up to the expected projections. It may be wise to liquidate your investment and move the money to a place that's more suitable. This process is called "cutting your losses." You should take this step only after asking lots of questions and receiving a great deal of information.

DCA accounts can be established with as little as $25 per month being invested. Each company sets its own "minimum investment" limits. Since the money is automatically taken from your bank account by the fund company, you don't see it, the money isn't in your hand, and you aren't tempted to spend it on things you really don't need. Dollar cost averaging accounts are great "forced investment" plans for people who aren't good at saving money on their own.

The 401(k) retirement plan presents a perfect example of dollar cost averaging. The money is deducted from your paycheck monthly and invested directly into a combination of investments selected by you. In many cases, your employer will match your contribution with company funds each time you invest. The funds accumulate on a tax-deferred basis—you pay no taxes on the accumulation until you withdraw the money at retirement time.

Consider Tom, a fast-rising manager in a large corporation. He's single, twenty-seven years old, and has been contributing to his 401(k) plan for four years. It's grown to more than $13,000 in that short period of time.

ADVICE FROM THE COACH: If you're not deducting from your paycheck the maximum amount allowed by your company to be invested in your 401(k) plan, *do it now!*

You won't like that smaller paycheck at first, and it will take a few months to adjust to the lower income, but when you're ready to retire, you'll be very thankful you contributed the maximum amount. Your retirement will be comfortable, and possibly more worry free.

Even if you don't have a 401(k) plan with your company, set up an individual retirement account (IRA) or a dollar cost averaging account today and begin a systematic investment program. When you're investing systematically, your account is earning interest. It's important to reinvest all interest and dividends unless you're retired and using the interest and/or dividends to supplement other retirement income. The interest and dividends roll back in to purchase additional shares, thus adding to the total number of shares that you own. The "Time Is Money" illustration that follows shows the magic of compound interest.

As you can see from the illustration, the sooner you begin your investment program, the greater your opportunity for more funds available at retirement.

Time Is Money

If you put aside	52¢
	8 hours a day
	7 days a week

You would be accumulating

$125 a month

$1,500 a year

If you put the money to work at

7 1/2% compounded continuously (7.9% effective annual yield)

For only 10 years, you will accumulate the following sums:

Deposit from ages	By age 65, you will have accumulated
0–10	$1,528,290
10–20	714,482
20–30	334,023
30–40	156,157
40–50	73,004
50–60	34,129
60–65 (5 years only)	9,476

Source: Reprinted with the permission of Simon & Schuster from *The Economics of Being a Woman* by Dee Dee Ahern and Betsy Bliss. Copyright © 1975 by Dee Dee Ahern and Betsy Bliss.

Buy and Hold

A very effective way to reduce investment risk is to invest for the long term. Ibbotson Associates, a financial consulting firm in Chicago, Illinois, looked at the performance of the stock market between 1926 and 1993. They used the Standard & Poors 500 Index as the measure of performance and measured every five-, ten-, and twenty-year period between 1926 and 1993. Here's what they learned:

During the five-year periods, the value of the stock increased in value 89 percent of the time. There were almost sixty five-year periods. Seven periods showed a loss, and four of these seven were during the Great Depression.

During the ten-year periods, stocks increased in value 97 percent of the time. There were almost fifty ten-year periods. Two losses occurred, both during the Great Depression.

When the holding period was increased to twenty years, stocks increased in value 100 percent of the time, and there were no losses. This included time during the Depression, major wars, inflation, and recession.

The longer you hold an investment, therefore, the better your chances for making a profit. Buy and hold. If you have a good company, a good money manager, and patience, you will be rewarded.

six

Coach's Corner:
Answers
to Common
Financial
Questions

As you begin taking steps to put your financial plan into action, you'll have to make decisions about certain "opportunities" or situations that arise. This chapter offers information that can guide you as you weigh your choices.

Learn the "Rule of 72"

The "Rule of 72" will tell you how long it takes for your money to double at various rates of compounding. For example, if an investment yields 10 percent, your money will double in 7.2 years ($72\div10=7.2$); if it yields 9 percent, your money will double in 8 years ($72\div9=8$); and so on. Coming at this from another angle, if you need your money to double in six years (e.g., to pay for college tuition), you will have to find an investment yielding 12 percent to achieve your goal ($72\div6=12$). Seventy-two is the "magic number" in making these calculations.

Question: Which Investment Would Be Better—6% Tax-exempt or 8% Taxable?

To answer this question, use this formula:

$$\frac{\text{Tax-Exempt Yield}}{1\text{-(your tax bracket)}} = \text{Tax Equivalent Yield}$$

Now, let's use real numbers. Assume the tax-exempt yield is 6 percent and your tax bracket is 28 percent.

$$\frac{6\%}{1\text{-}28\%} = x$$

$$\frac{6\%}{1\text{-}.28 = .72} = 8.33\% \text{ Tax Equivalent Yield}$$

Conclusion: For the purposes of this example, if your investment earns more than 8.33 percent, the taxable investment may be your best choice.

Bulls and Bears: What's It All About?

Have you heard about the "running of the bulls" in Pamplona, Spain? The bulls are let loose to run through the streets as fearless people run ahead of them, hoping to keep out of their way. When the stock market is moving ahead with the prices of most (but not necessarily all) stocks rising, this is referred to as a "bullish" market. The volume of stocks traded is usually heavy, and the action of investors buying stocks tends to push prices upwards.

A "bear" market happens when things are sluggish (think of a bear about to go into hibernation). Few investors seem to be interested in buying. Trading volumes are lower and market prices remain flat or decline.

Bull and bear markets may indicate how investors feel about the future. In a bear market, the investors may be pessimistic or gloomy about the future and content to stay where they are. Investors in a bull market create frenzied stock buying because they are optimistic about their country's economy and the performance of different market segments.

ADVICE FROM THE COACH: How do you invest in these markets for gain? Buy and hold! Don't worry about bull markets. If you are investing for the long term, chances are you'll reach your financial goals.

Find a money manager:

- With a good track record.
- That you can trust.
- That doesn't "churn" your account (make a lot of trades to generate commissions).
- Who charges reasonable fees.
- Whose advice is in your best interest.
- Who invests for long periods of time.

What to Look for in a Good Investment Program

To determine if an investment is right for you, use the following questions as your measuring stick:

1. **Is it professionally managed?** Is it managed by experts with at least ten years' experience managing portfolios of money?

2. **Is it constantly supervised?** Do the experts give all their attention to the money portfolio? Do they have the best research and tools available from Wall Street?

3. **Is it diversified?** Does it offer a variety of least twenty-five different investment issues from different industries and issuers to reduce risk if a downturn occurs in any one investment group?

4. Is it flexible? Can I change from one investment portfolio group to another to accommodate changes in my lifestyle and needs?

5. How quickly can it be liquidated? Can the investment (or a portion) be readily turned into cash should my financial circumstances change?

6. Is it low cost? Does the investment program offer investments that provide maximum benefits without high or unnecessary fees?

Try to find investments that allow you to answer "yes" to all of these questions.

Greed Is a Nasty Word

Buyer beware—pay attention to those words! You'll have many opportunities to part with your hard-earned money in investments that claim "We'll make you rich overnight."

There are so-called foundations in which you buy a membership (costing $400 to $500) that supposedly puts you on the receiving end of information you can use to allegedly double or triple your income in a very short period of time.

The seminar leaders are seductive—getting you caught up in a vision of newfound wealth and opulence. You rush to the back of the room to plunk down your credit card and you're on your way to prosperity. Those who attend these so-called "wealth-building" seminars never stop to think that the leaders make their *real* money from the sale of books and tapes at the back of the room and from the efforts of their highly trained telephone crews (highly trained in sales, not investments) who will later go into action and call you to part with *more* of your hard-earned money (for their "custom" insurance policies and investment programs).

DON'T GO TO THE SEMINARS!

DON'T SPEND YOUR MONEY!

DON'T LISTEN TO THEM!

The observation has been that people who get caught up in these types of programs have let greed take over their common sense. And most of these people have absolutely no business taking part in these programs—they can't afford it, but they do it because the greed factor is overwhelming.

These schemes almost never work. And most of these programs don't work either. But avarice can completely cloud judgment.

Years ago a former securities commissioner of a Midwestern state related that people in his state sent thousands upon thousands of dollars to a post office box (first red flag) in a foreign country (second red flag) because someone proclaimed that he had successfully crossed a mink and a snake...and every spring the mink shed its skin!

And in a courtroom several years ago, the defendant, on trial for securities fraud, told the jury, "The higher the interest rates I promised, the more money the investors sent me." He had almost gotten up to a promised annual rate of return of 100 percent.

Greed *is* a nasty word. Don't let it get you. Sometimes it hits when you're desperate, or when you feel "lucky." Turn around and walk the other way. The pipe dream won't follow because it's too busy looking for the next sucker.

Contingency Day Planning

In her book *Being a Widow*, Lynn Caine posed an excellent suggestion: Once a year, all couples should sit down and declare a Contingency Day—an annual review of the family's finances. The partners would sit down together and discuss the following subjects:

- Wills (Each partner should have a separate will)

- Life insurance (Who is the agent? Is the coverage whole life, term, universal life? Are there any loans on the policies?)

- Pensions (Who do you contact for questions on the plan? Are there survivor benefits if the covered person dies before age 65?)

- Mortgage insurance

- Retirement (What are the plans for living? What are your goals?)

- Family bank accounts (Which bank or banks? Checking? Savings? Safe deposit box location and number?)

- Stocks, bonds, securities (What kind? Are they in street name?* Who is the broker?)

- Real estate (Any owned in another state?)

- Debts (Anyone owe you money? Do you owe any money?)

- Steps to be taken if either of you should die within the next twelve months

- How much money the surviving partner would have to live on

- How much money the surviving partner would need to live on

- Changes in lifestyle that would be necessary

* "Street name" means that the brokerage company retains the stock certificates in its name but they *do* belong to you. Keeping stocks in street name makes it easier to sell the stocks when you need the cash. If you keep the stock certificates, you will have to safeguard them as they are as good as cash. It is better to keep stocks in street name for ease of liquidity and protection against theft.

Ms. Caine notes that one of the partners may refuse to join in the Contingency Day planning—it might be too uncomfortable. If that's the case, you can go ahead and do it on your own. You might write a letter that will inform your partner, financial coach, and attorney about anything not contained in the will.

Make this special day an annual event, preferably on a birthday or anniversary. What a lovely gift to give your partner to show that you care. The accompanying Personal Document checklist serves as a terrific tool in this roundup.

Personal Document
Checklist and Locator
SAMPLE

	Yes	No	Location
Birth certificate(s)	___	___	_____
Passport(s)	___	___	_____
Marriage certificate	___	___	_____
Divorce decree	___	___	_____
Social security card(s)	___	___	_____
Death certificate(s)	___	___	_____
Will(s)	___	___	_____
Trust documents	___	___	_____
Real estate deeds and mortgages	___	___	_____
Tax returns (last seven years)	___	___	_____
Homeowners/renters insurance policy	___	___	_____
Life insurance policies	___	___	_____
Medical insurance policies	___	___	_____
Disability insurance policies	___	___	_____
Car insurance policies	___	___	_____
Other insurance policies	___	___	_____
Employee benefit/pension records	___	___	_____
Retirement plan	___	___	_____
IRA/Keogh/SEP/IRA documents	___	___	_____

Stock certificates   ___   ___   _____

Bonds   ___   ___   _____

Brokerage account statements   ___   ___   _____

Mutual fund statements   ___   ___   _____

Annuities   ___   ___   _____

Bank statements   ___   ___   _____

Safe deposit box information   ___   ___   _____

Car registration information   ___   ___   _____

Other: ___   ___   _____

_____   ___   ___   _____

_____   ___   ___   _____

_____   ___   ___   _____

_____   ___   ___   _____

_____   ___   ___   _____

_____   ___   ___   _____

Pay for Everything by Check

One of the best ways to keep track of your finances is to pay by check. Open a bank account with free check-writing privileges and make all your payments by check. If your child needs money for school pictures, pay by check. Need money for Cub Scouts? Pay by check. Give any child selling candy a check for the amount—you'll have accurate records of all donations that are tax deductible. It's an easy way to keep track of all expenditures.

Every time you buy anything with cash—a drink, an ice cream cone, a newspaper—get a receipt. Keep all these receipts in a business envelope that you carry with you at all times. If you give someone a tip or money but can't get a receipt, write the date, the amount of the tip, and what it was for on the envelope itself. Each day when you put a receipt in the envelope, put it in the back of the stack. That way at the end of the week when you pull out all your receipts, they will be in order by date. Carry a new envelope each week and you will have a complete and accurate record of all your expenses. That's being a smart money manager!

seven

Choosing the Right Coach

As in athletics, there are many different kinds of coaches in financial planning. However, although a football coach would not train gymnasts, and a golf instructor would not teach swimming, in the financial world there are individuals who will coach you in all aspects of financial planning—insurance, investments, taxes, law, and so forth. These financial coaches are generalists, not specialists, and they can be very helpful. Still, it's important that you check out their credentials—that you interview them. Following is a format for making an informed selection.

- *Find out your prospect's level of education.* What degrees does he or she have? And in what field?

- *What life insurance licenses does he or she have?*

  ☐ Life

  ☐ Disability

  ☐ Property and casualty

- *What securities licenses does he or she have?*

  ☐ NASD (National Association of Securities Dealers) Series 6—a three-hour exam that limits a broker to selling mutual funds

  ☐ NASD Series 7—a six-hour general securities exam that allows a broker to sell all securities

  ☐ NASD Series 63—allows the person to sell in multiple states

  ☐ NASD Series 24—registered principal exam—allows the person to hire, manage, and assume responsibility for other securities licensed people

  ☐ Variable annuity license

  A salesperson can only recommend to you those products for which he or she is properly licensed. This limits the recommendations the person can make for you. For example, a broker with just a Series 6 license can only suggest that you invest in mutual funds.

- *Has he or she earned any designations?*

  ☐ CPA—Certified Public Accountant

  ☐ EA—Enrolled Agent

  ☐ CTP—Certified Tax Preparer

  ☐ CFP—Certified Financial Planner

  ☐ CLU—Chartered Life Underwriter

  ☐ ChFC—Chartered Financial Consultant

  Such designations are earned through additional education and testing by examination. There are many more designations, but those listed above are the most common and the best known. Be on your guard with other so-called titles and designations—they may sound legitimate, but some can be attained through just a one- or two-day course and a fee.

- *To what associations does your prospect belong?*

  ☐ Securities Industry Association

  ☐ International Association for Financial Planning

  ☐ Institute of Certified Financial Planners

  ☐ Life Underwriters Association

  ☐ Chartered Life Underwriters

  ☐ American Institute of Certified Public Accountants

  Write down the organizations to which the potential coach belongs and research them at the library by asking for the book entitled *Encyclopedia of Industry Associations*. Find out if there's a local chapter of the group. Does the potential coach attend the chapter meetings? How often does he or she attend industry conferences? Is it necessary to earn continuing education credits in order to maintain his or her designation? Does he or she keep abreast of what's happening in the industry?

A financial coach can only advise you about insurance or investments if he or she is licensed by the state (insurance) or the NASD (securities). If you are being advised about a specific investment, the coach must present you with a prospectus. If the prospectus is not presented, don't even think about putting your money in the investment. The presentation about the product may not be lawful. The advisor also cannot (by law) underline, circle, or highlight any line or sentence in the prospectus.

Some financial coaches are called "fee-only" planners. They have no licenses and do not receive commissions from the sale of products. Instead, they will charge you a fee for their financial planning and recommendations, but it's up to you to do the investments, usually through a discount brokerage firm. It really doesn't matter whether your coach is a fee-and-commission or fee-only advisor. What matters is that you have a good rapport and that he or she listens to your needs and helps you formulate the plans to reach your goals.

 ADVICE FROM THE COACH: Some fee-only coaches may recommend a service called "asset allocation." In this coach's opinion, here's a lawsuit waiting to happen. The coach takes your money for investment and "allocates" percentages of it into no-load mutual funds. For years, the experts who study funds on a twenty-four-hour basis and move money in and out depending on what's happening in the market haven't been very successful. Why, then, do these planners who do asset allocation using less sophisticated techniques and software (having less research than the experts) think they can do a better job of it? Asset allocation will be successful as long as the stock market holds up. But the minute the market takes a downturn, clients will be furious when they see their losses, and the lawsuits will begin. Incidentally, you pay a fairly substantial annual fee for asset allocation.

If you have a substantial amount of money and want to have it professionally managed, place it with a firm that has done professional money management for at least thirty years. The same firm in Boston, Massachusetts, is still managing Ben Franklin's two-hundred-year trust! Look for longevity in the business and good manager/client communication, not the planner next door who now does asset allocation. It doesn't matter if he or she has had a 100 percent return in the last five years—it isn't worth taking the risk.

People who offer investment advice must register with the Securities and Exchange Commission (SEC). You have the right to ask them for a copy of their Form ADV (Uniform Application for Investment Advisor Registration). This form will tell you:

- With what companies they are affiliated.

- Their fee schedule.

- How they derive their income (what percentages come from fees, commission, insurance, securities, etc.).

- Their educational and employment history.

- The type of products they recommend.

When interviewing investment advisors, you'll want to obtain a list of references. Call them! You should ask the reference the following questions:

- How well do you know the advisor?

- How often do you meet with the advisor?

- How knowledgeable are you about financial planning?

- How did you learn about this advisor?

- What do you like best about this advisor?

- What don't you like about this advisor?

- How much better is your financial position today from when you first met with this advisor?

If you get any "I don't really know" answers, start looking for another advisor.

The professional financial advisor will be in constant touch with his or her clients (mostly by mail) to keep them advised on their financial position. In addition, the advisor should meet with clients no less than annually to bring them up to date on their financial status—to deliver good *and* bad news. Communication is vital in an advisor/client relationship.

How to Find Money for Investing

"I don't have any money for investment." If financial coaches have heard this statement once, they've heard it a million times. It's not that you're not earning enough money—it's that you're spending too much on the wrong things! Think of saving as spending. Each dollar you earn should be working for you—think of it as your employee. Therefore, put as many employees to work for you as you can—the salary they earn, they send to you!

In this chapter, you will encounter many ideas for finding money to invest. It's there, waiting for you to make it work for you—all you have to do is spend a couple of hours looking for it. You have a big treasure chest filled with places to find money. Lift up the lid and start looking.

Finding Money for Investment: A Treasure Chest of Ideas

1. Spend half of what you usually spend for entertainment. Go out once or twice a month instead of four times a month.

2. If you *have* to see that hit movie, go to a matinée—the price is lower. Or wait until it hits the dollar movie theaters. Put your savings in a piggy bank.

3. Have a garage sale. Invest the proceeds.

4. Take the clothes you no longer wear and sell them through a consignment shop.

5. Work overtime, or get a second job on Saturdays. Put 80 percent of the extra money in savings and spend 20 percent on yourself.

6. Buy generic drugs when appropriate—your costs can be reduced as much as 30 percent. For maintenance drugs, ask the pharmacist if you can get a discount for buying in larger quantities.

7. Drive within the speed limit. If you get a speeding ticket, your insurance costs may rise dramatically. Drive safely to keep your insurance premiums down.

8. In twenty-nine states and Washington, D.C., you may be able to get a discount on your car insurance if you have taken a defensive driver course.

9. If you're 55 or over, many restaurants offer a senior menu with lower prices. The portions may be slightly smaller but still adequate, and you don't need all that food anyway!

10. People 55 or over also get a substantial (almost 50 percent) discount at many movie theaters.

11. Save money on moving. Pack the stuff yourself—you can save about 10 percent. Move on a week day—the costs are lower than weekends.

12. Consider buying gas appliances. In many areas, electricity costs are much higher than gas. Do your research. Examine the costs of switching over to gas, including the cost (usually higher) of the appliances. Over the long term, the lower monthly bills may be worth the conversion costs.

13. Turn off lights as you leave a room. It's amazing how much money you'll free up for investment by adopting this good habit.

14. Take a "Navy" shower. Get yourself wet. Turn off the water, soap yourself, and then turn the water back on to rinse off.

15. Do the same when you brush your teeth. Wet the brush, turn off the water, brush, and then turn the water on to rinse the brush.

16. Don't peel potatoes, carrots, and other vegetables under running water. Put a pan of water in the sink and use it to rinse the vegetables as you peel them.

17. Instead of going away on a weekend, ship the kids to grandma's, turn off the phone, and go out to dinner. You won't have a hotel bill. Do this with another family with children. Give each other an "adult" weekend.

18. Drink water at restaurants instead of other beverages you have to pay for.

19. Wash your laundry in cold water. The clothes get just as clean, and you'll save hot water costs.

20. Send a fax instead of making a long-distance call.

21. Send long-distance faxes after 5:00 p.m. when rates are lower.

22. Buy the refill container of juice, laundry detergent, and so forth. The refills usually cost less per ounce than the regular package.

23. Collect aluminum cans. Put the cash you receive into savings.

24. Shop at factory outlet and surplus stores. You may save 30 to 70 percent on clothing and other articles. Get on the stores' mailing lists for sales and save even more!

25. Don't rent your telephones. Buy them!

26. Raise your insurance deductibles. Invest in savings what you save on premium payments.

27. Take care of your clothing. Hang up good suits and dresses with zippers zipped and covered with plastic dry cleaner bags. Your clothes will last longer and you can invest the money you *don't* need for new clothes. Buy classic articles that never go out of style, no matter what the latest fad.

28. Buy washable fabrics—you'll save on dry cleaning bills.

29. Use clean empty juice cans for kids' building blocks. The juice is good for the kids, and they love building big castles and forts with the cans.

30. Lower the thermostat and save on heating bills.

31. Write a letter instead of calling long distance.

32. Don't go to a car wash. Wash the car yourself—the exercise is good for you!

33. Buy used books instead of new ones. Better yet, get them at the library.

34. Recognize when you feel a "buy-itis" fit coming on and do something else so you won't spend money.

35. Get your car serviced regularly—you'll save on gas and repair bills over the long term.

36. Know what you want *before* you go shopping. Set a limit for each of your purchases.

37. Eat out less. Cook in large quantities and freeze for future meals.

38. Drive an economy car. Payments, gas, repairs, and insurance cost less for cars in this class.

39. Take your lunch to work. Write on your lunch bag how much money you're saving by not going out to lunch—you'll feel proud of yourself.

40. Check out swap meets, flea markets, and garage sales for good buys.

41. Turn off your television. You'll be amazed at how often you leave the set on even though you're not watching.

42. Use your dishwasher every other day instead of every day. Better yet, run it only when it's full.

43. Eat before you go grocery shopping—you'll buy less.

44. Cook extra food and freeze it so you can pop it in the microwave on nights when you're in a hurry and tempted to go out for fast food.

45. Cook in your microwave oven. It costs less to use a microwave than an electric or gas oven.

46. Be a coupon clipper, but buy only what you need.

47. Can't resist using your credit card? Put it in a dish of water and put the dish in the freezer. The card is tough to use when it's in the middle of a block of ice.

48. Buy clothes at a consignment shop. Many designer items are worn only once by "celebrities" who can't be seen wearing the same outfit twice. You'll get some excellent buys and look great.

49. Do your research. Buying even a single share of stock in some companies can get you discounts. Look into such companies as Radio Shack, Marriott, General Mills, and Disneyland.

50. Use cloth diapers. You may save $300 a year. Put your savings into an account for the baby's college education.

51. Get your hair cut every six weeks instead of every month. You can save over $100 a year.

52. Have your bank checks printed through an independent company that offers lower prices.

53. Mix whole milk with half powdered milk.

54. Get together with neighbors and send electric, gas, and water bills in one envelope to each company. You'll see lots of postage savings.

55. Share babysitting duties with someone else who has children.

56. Step on your toilet tissue rolls. When you flatten the roll, children can't unroll the tissue as easily. The roll will last longer.

57. If you have to go out for coffee at work, chip in with three or four other employees and buy a $14.95 coffee maker, coffee, and supplies. You can save almost $30 a week.

58. You can save on heating costs by making sure that the fireplace damper is always closed when not in use.

59. Eliminate life insurance coverage for kids. They don't need it. Invest the money in a good growth mutual fund.

60. Eat your large meal at lunch. The food is cheaper.

61. Instead of ordering an entreé for dinner at a restaurant, order two appetizers. The cost is less and the amount of food is substantial.

62. Need money to send the kids to college? Marianne Ragins received more than $400,000 in college scholarship funds and wrote the book *Winning Scholarships for College* to tell you how she did it.

63. Shop alone. You have a better chance of sticking to your prepared grocery list. Kids, spouses, and significant others have a habit of slipping candy bars, toys, and gourmet items into the grocery cart or talking you into buying items on impulse.

64. Buy store-brand items when possible. You can save significantly, as these examples show:

Flour (5 lbs.)	$.30
Sugar (5 lbs.)	$.60
Salt (1 lb.)	$.09
Vinegar (1 qt.)	$.60
Bleach (2 qts.)	$.40

Over the course of a year, the savings add up.

65. Water your lawn and garden at night. During the day, much of the water evaporates before it does much good. Watering at night significantly cuts back on the amount of water needed.

66. Shop at appliance, furniture, and houseware stores at the end of the month. If the store hasn't met its monthly quota, it may be inclined to sell items at reduced prices.

67. Buy next year's holiday cards, gift wrap, decorations, lights, and so on the day after Christmas. You'll enjoy reductions of 50 percent or more.

68. Put gas in your car early in the morning. You'll get as much as five percent more before the sun's heat has expanded the gas in the service station's fuel tank.

69. Take the bus once a week to work. Put the money you save on gas in an investment account. Your car will last longer too.

70. When making hotel reservations, save money by calling the hotel directly. The 800-number reservations office will frequently quote a higher rate.

71. Always check your grocery store and credit card bills. It's been estimated that over 40 percent of customer bills contain errors.

72. Buy large home maintenance items such as lawnmowers, snowblowers, and so on with a trusted neighbor. You'll cut your costs 50 percent. The same goes for sewing machines, power tools, and magazine subscriptions.

73. Don't go to a hit movie at the theater. Wait until it comes out on video. You'll enjoy more than a 50 percent savings on the movie and 90 percent savings on the sodas, popcorn, and candy.

74. To save on college costs, have the student establish a new residence in the state where the college is located so you can qualify for the lower in-state tuition. This idea can save you as much as $20,000 over a four-year period.

75. Buy postage stamps by mail. The post office pays postage both ways, and you save on gas.

76. Save money on a fitness club membership by volunteering to work in the child care room. Many fitness clubs will give a free membership in exchange for your child care services a few hours a week. Take your kids with you.

77. Save money on clothes by checking your local dry cleaner. Some will sell clothes they've held for sixty days or more. Often, they'll sell them at the dry cleaning price.

78. Have minor car dents and collision repairs fixed by students at a local vocational school. There's usually no labor charge, and you may only have to pay for paint and parts.

79. Rather than buy a new cookbook, exchange recipes with neighbors, friends, or relatives. Or check out the "Food" section of your local newspaper. Also watch for the coupon supplements that come in the mail or with the newspaper. Often the products the coupons are valid for are featured in an accompanying recipe.

80. Don't charge your at-home college kids rent. Have them pay the electric or phone bills. They'll start turning off the lights and making shorter phone calls.

81. To cut down on Christmas gift giving, draw names within the family. Invest the money as a gift to you.

82. Instead of giving someone a store-bought gift, give a roll of your favorite cookie dough. They can freeze it, slice it, and bake at will. Families in which both parents work will appreciate this type of gift.

83. Wash clothes every day so you don't have to buy as many clothes.

84. If you get a traffic ticket, go to court. The judge may accept your explanation and reduce or eliminate the fine.

85. If you're a commuter, check with your employer to see if the company offers transit subsidies to employees who use public transportation.

86. Team up with co-workers who must commute to work and purchase large quantities of mass transit passes for a discount.

87. If you buy a new vehicle, make sure you're charged the local tax for the area in which you live, not the area in which the dealership is located. The difference in the tax could be as much as $150.

88. Save money on monthly cable television charges by first trying an amplified indoor antenna (powered rabbit ears). Save the receipt to return it if they don't work.

89. Save money on moving costs by shipping some items, such as books, by mail, UPS, or bus.

90. Buy the economy size of household cleaners. Save the original container and just buy the refill package when you're out of the cleaner. You'll not only save money on the product, you'll be helping the environment by reducing the amount of packaging you throw away.

91. Save money by changing your eating habits. Avoid buying high-priced junk foods, and remember, you'll pay more for prepackaged ready-to-eat items. Prepare as much food from scratch as time allows.

92. If you travel in your job, collect all the soap, shampoo, and mouthwash in your hotel rooms. You've paid for them in your room fee.

93. Buy your next load of wood for the fireplace from the woodworking department at your school. They give away or sell the wood scraps. It's much cheaper than buying regular firewood or pressed logs, and it burns just as well.

94. Save money on school lunches by putting sandwiches in washable (and reusable) plastic containers. Use a cloth napkin and buy the lunch container at a yard sale.

95. Have a new baby? Check with local hospitals to see if they have programs that allow you to "borrow" car seats. Also, don't be tempted by some of the high-priced baby gadgets that you may rarely use.

96. At the end of the day, place the coins in your purse or pocket in a jar. Today's loose change is tomorrow's investment dollars.

97. Save money on clothing and furniture by cruising student housing complexes near colleges and universities. Students often sell items cheaply after they graduate.

98. To save on child care costs, ask a college student you trust to watch your children in exchange for free use of your washer and dryer.

99. Stop smoking! Enough said.

100. Want other money-saving ideas? Read *The Tightwad Gazette* and *The Tightwad Gazette II* by Amy Dacyczyn.

Additional Suggestions

Another strategy involves dividing your salary into "piles." Try allocating your paycheck in the following manner:

Week 1 Use this portion to pay your bills.

Week 2 Use this portion for loan payments (car, college, computer, etc.).

Week 3 Use this portion for rent or mortgage.

Week 4 Use this portion for savings (half) and entertainment (half).

Week 5 Every fourth month you'll get an "extra" paycheck. Put it into savings. (Spend 20 percent on yourself as a reward if you meet the goals stated in the rest of the plan.)

Even modest adjustments to your lifestyle and spending habits can produce real investment capital. Here are some examples of how to cut down on expenses to free up money for savings:

Current Monthly Spending	New Monthly Spending	Savings for Investment
Food (cook from scratch)		
$400	$300	$100
Entertainment (rent videos)		
$400	$200	$200
Telephone (fax or write letters)		
$150	$125	$25
Gas—home (wear a sweater)		
$25	$20	$5
Electricity (turn off lights)		
$60	$55	$5

Auto (walk to store)

| $80 | $75 | $5 |

Gifts (buy cheap and tasty)

| $80 | $75 | $5 |

Charity (begins at home)

| $40 | $30 | $10 |

Personal grooming (do more yourself)

| $60 | $50 | $10 |

Clothing (shop at consignment stores)

| $100 | $50 | $50 |

Vacations (stay at home)

| $100 | $50 | $50 |

Child care (share with neighbors)

| $50 | $20 | $30 |

Household supplies (buy economy)

| $50 | $30 | $20 |

| $1,595 | $1,080 | $515 |

Just by cutting down on phone calls, turning off lights, and sharing baby-sitting duties, you can find money for investing. Now it's your turn! Use Warm-Up Exercise #9 to find ways to save money for investing.

Warm-up Exercise Nine

Finding Money to Invest

Use this worksheet to examine your lifestyle and find areas where you can cut back and invest the savings. Extra space has been provided for you to account for areas of spending not listed here. However, items such as rent, mortgage, car payments, and life or medical insurance aren't included because they may be fixed payments or essential to your well-being. But you have many other areas where you can find money for future financial goals.

	Current Spending Amounts	New Spending Amounts	Savings for Investment
Food	_____	_____	_____
Entertainment	_____	_____	_____
Telephone	_____	_____	_____
Gas (home)	_____	_____	_____
Electricity	_____	_____	_____
Auto	_____	_____	_____
Gifts	_____	_____	_____
Charity	_____	_____	_____
Personal grooming	_____	_____	_____
Clothing	_____	_____	_____
Vacation	_____	_____	_____

Child care   _____   _____   _____

Household supplies   _____   _____   _____

Other:

_____   _____   _____   _____

_____   _____   _____   _____

_____   _____   _____   _____

_____   _____   _____   _____

_____   _____   _____   _____

_____   _____   _____   _____

_____   _____   _____   _____

Totals   _____   _____   _____

Life-Stage Goals

When considering your "big picture" financially, it's helpful (and practical) to tailor your goals to correspond to stages in your life, as in the following example:

Age 20-30
Start a systematic savings plan for growth

Establish credit

Pay off college loans

Write a will

Age 30-40
Set up a college fund for children

Buy a home

Start a retirement plan

Age 40-50
Put as much as possible in savings

Get kids (or self) through college

Update wills

Decide when to change portfolio objectives

Age 50-60
Own home free and clear

Change investments to produce income

Make sure medical and elder care coverages are adequate

Make retirement plans and set new goals

Age 60 and up
Live on golden pond, not olden pond

Keep wills current

Shift assets to lower taxes on estate

Travel and love life

Glossary

Aggressive growth stocks. Stocks that can increase in value or lose value very rapidly.

Annuity. A contract sold by insurance companies that guarantees a fixed or variable payment to the annuity holder at some time in the future, usually at retirement.

Assets. Anything having value (house, car, furniture, stocks, bonds, mutual funds, etc.).

Bond. Any interest-bearing or discounted government security that obligates the issuer to pay the bondholder a specified sum of money and to repay the principal amount at maturity.

Broker (insurance). A person who finds the best insurance deal for the client and then sells the policy to the client.

Broker (real estate). The person who represents the seller in the property transaction, earning a commission on the sale.

Broker (securities). The person who is the liaison between the buyer and the seller, charging a commission for services.

Capital Appreciation Mutual Funds. A fund in which all income earned by the fund is invested back into the fund for more rapid growth.

Certificates of deposit (CD). An investment issued by a bank that usually pays interest.

Commodities. Goods in bulk (grains, metals, foods, etc.) that are traded on a commodities exchange.

Deductible. The amount not covered by insurance and which the policy owner would have to pay.

Disability insurance. Insurance that pays a person income upon disability (inability to work).

Dollar cost averaging. Investing a fixed amount of money in securities every month or at set intervals.

Emergency fund. Funds accumulated in a bank account that is used only to pay bills when income is not coming from other sources such as employment.

Government securities. Securities issued by the U.S. government (Treasury bills, bonds, notes, savings bonds, etc.). They are backed by the full faith and credit of the U.S. government.

Junk bonds. High-risk bonds with a lower credit rating.

Liabilities. Assets a person owns but on which the owner owes money (car, home, etc.).

Limited partnership. An investment created by a general partner who manages a variety of properties for the investors (Limited Partners).

Living trust. Known as "inter-vivos trust." This trust is set up between individuals during their lifetime but does not become effective until the trustor (person establishing the trust) dies.

Minimum investment limit. The smallest amount of money an investor may invest in the investment.

Money market fund. An investment composed of a variety of highly liquid and safe securities (commercial paper, bankers acceptances, government securities, etc.). These pay slightly higher than bank interest rates.

Mortgage. A debt instrument showing the borrower (homeowner) how much is owed the lender (bank, loan company).

Mutual fund. The pooling of funds contributed by investors to manage a portfolio of stocks, bonds, and so forth by a professional money manager.

Net worth. The total value of all possessions (house, stocks, bonds, etc.) minus all outstanding debts (loans, bills, mortgage, etc.)

Options. Securities transaction agreements tied to stocks, commodities, or stock indexes and which are traded on stock exchanges.

Precious metals. Gold, platinum, magnesium, silver, and so on.

Principal. The basic amount invested, exclusive of earnings.

Professionally managed proceeds. The amount of money managed by a person who has many years of experience managing money for corporations and individuals.

Profit sharing. An agreement between a corporation and its employees that allows employees to share in the company profits.

Prospectus. Official written contract for buying an investment. It specifies the objectives, risks, expenses, and management.

Public assistance. Payments made to individuals who are in need because they cannot get work or are unable to work.

Purchasing power. The value of money as measured by the goods and services it can buy.

Risk management. The establishment of an insurance program that would make payments for loss of life, home, property, and so on, thus reducing risk of financial hardship.

Royalty income. Income paid to a holder for the right to use property such as a patent, copyrighted material, or natural resources.

Tax deferred. An investment whose accumulated earnings are free from taxation until the investor takes possession of them.

Tax exempt. An investment whose interest is free from taxation by federal, state, and local authorities.

U.S. Treasury Bill. Commonly called a T-Bill. An investment issued by the government. It has a high degree of safety and liquidity. The yield may barely exceed the rate of inflation.

Unit investment trusts. An investment that purchases a fixed portfolio of income-producing securities. Unit holders receive an undivided interest in both the principal and the income portion of the portfolio in proportion to the amount of money they invest.

Workers' compensation. Income paid to an employee who is disabled and unable to work on the job.

Bibliography

Armstrong, Alexandra, and Mary R. Donahue. *On Your Own: A Widow's Passage to Emotional and Financial Well-Being*. Chicago: Dearborn Financial Publishing, 1993.

Bender, Martin S. *Everyone Needs a Will*. Holbrook, MA: Bob Adams, 1990.

Boroson, Warren. *Keys to Investing in Your 401(k)*. Hauppauge, NY: Barron's Educational Services, 1994.

Caine, Lynn. *Being a Widow*. New York: Arbor House, 1988.

Chilton, David. *The Wealthy Barber: Everyone's Common-Sense Guide to Becoming Financially Independent*. Rocklin, CA: Prima Publishing, 1991.

Clason, George, S. *The Richest Man in Babylon*. New York: Hawthorn, 1955.

Crumbley, D. Larry, and L. Murphy Smith. *Keys to Personal Financial Planning*. Hauppauge, NY: Barron's Educational Services, 1994.

Dacyczyn, Amy. *The Tightwad Gazette: Promoting Thrift as a Viable Alternative Lifestyle*. New York: Villard Books, 1993.

Dacyczyn, Amy. *The Tightwad Gazette II: Promoting Thrift as a Viable Alternative Lifestyle*. New York: Villard Books, 1995.

Dalton, Robb E. *Lifeplanning*. Phoenix, AZ: D.M. Wordsmith, 1987.

Deaton, Dennis R. *Money: An Owner's Manual*. Phoenix, AZ: TimeMax, 1992.

Dolan, Ken, and Daria Dolan. *The Smart Money Family Financial Planner*. New York: Berkley Books, 1992.

Fisher, Mark. *The Instant Millionaire*. San Rafael, CA: New World Library, 1990.

Fullner, Wanda. *A Primer on Personal Money Management for Midlife and Older Women*. Washington, DC: AARP, 1992.

Hedrick, Lucy. *365 Ways to Save Money*. New York: Hearst Books, 1994.

Nadler, Beverly. *Success Through Self-Confidence*. New York: Random House, 1988.

Ortalda, Robert A., Jr. *Financial Sanity: How to Live Within Your Means and Still Finance Your Dreams*. New York: Doubleday, 1989.

Pond, Jonathan D., Michael A. Dalton, and O'Neill Wyss. *The ABCs of Managing Your Money*. Denver, CO: National Endowment for Financial Education, 1993.

Ragins, Marianne. *Winning Scholarships for College: An Insider's Guide*. New York: Henry Holt, 1994.

Simmons, Lee, and Barbara Simmons. *Penny Pinching*. New York: Bantam, 1991.

Tyson, Eric. *Personal Finance for Dummie$*. San Mateo, CA: IDG Books Worldwide, 1994.

Ungar, Alan B. *Financial Self-Confidence for the Suddenly Single*. Los Angeles: Lowell House, 1989.

Whitlock, Charles R. *Easy Money*. New York: Kensington Books, 1994.

Woodhouse, Violet, Victoria Felton-Collins, and M.C. Blakeman. *Divorce and Money: How to Make the Best Financial Decisions During Divorce*. Berkeley, CA: Nolo Press, 1993.

Young, Fred J. *How to Get Rich and Stay Rich*. Hollywood, FL: Lifetime Books, 1992.

Available From SkillPath Publications

Self-Study Sourcebooks

Climbing the Corporate Ladder: What You Need to Know and Do to Be a Promotable Person *by Barbara Pachter and Marjorie Brody*

Coping With Supervisory Nightmares: 12 Common Nightmares of Leadership and What You Can Do About Them *by Michael and Deborah Singer Dobson*

Defeating Procrastination: 52 Fail-Safe Tips for Keeping Time on Your Side *by Marlene Caroselli, Ed.D.*

Discovering Your Purpose *by Ivy Haley*

Going for the Gold: Winning the Gold Medal for Financial Independence *by Lesley D. Bissett, CFP*

Having Something to Say When You Have to Say Something: The Art of Organizing Your Presentation *by Randy Horn*

Info-Flood: How to Swim in a Sea of Information Without Going Under *by Marlene Caroselli, Ed.D.*

The Innovative Secretary *by Marlene Caroselli, Ed.D.*

Letters & Memos: Just Like That! *by Dave Davies*

Mastering the Art of Communication: Your Keys to Developing a More Effective Personal Style *by Michelle Fairfield Poley*

Obstacle Illusions: Coverting Crisis to Opportunity *by Marlene Caroselli, Ed.D.*

Organized for Success! 95 Tips for Taking Control of Your Time, Your Space, and Your Life *by Nanci McGraw*

A Passion to Lead! How to Develop Your Natural Leadership Ability *by Michael Plumstead*

P.E.R.S.U.A.D.E.: Communication Strategies That Move People to Action *by Marlene Caroselli, Ed.D.*

Productivity Power: 250 Great Ideas for Being More Productive *by Jim Temme*

Promoting Yourself: 50 Ways to Increase Your Prestige, Power, and Paycheck *by Marlene Caroselli, Ed.D.*

Proof Positive: How to Find Errors Before They Embarrass You *by Karen L. Anderson*

Risk-Taking: 50 Ways to Turn Risks Into Rewards *by Marlene Caroselli, Ed.D. and David Harris*

Stress Control: How You Can Find Relief From Life's Daily Stress *by Steve Bell*

The Technical Writer's Guide *by Robert McGraw*

Total Quality Customer Service: How to Make It Your Way of Life *by Jim Temme*

Write It Right! A Guide for Clear and Correct Writing *by Richard Andersen and Helene Hinis*

Your Total Communication Image *by Janet Signe Olson, Ph.D.*

Handbooks

The ABC's of Empowered Teams: Building Blocks for Success *by Mark Towers*

For more information, call 1-800-873-7545.

Notes

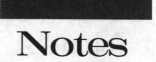

Notes

Notes

Notes